To Larry & Sharon
with lots of love from the L.E.F.C. Nov. 2:7
Bible Study group —

The Lighter Side of Church Life

Mary
Penny
Shelley
Bev.

The Lighter Side
of **Church Life**

Tyndale House Publishers, Inc.
Wheaton, Illinois

ISBN 0-8423-2855-6
Copyright 1988 by Christianity Today, Inc.
All rights reserved
Printed in the United States of America

95   94   93   92

10   9   8   7   6   5   4

CONTENTS

Part I. Congregations

Part II. Pastors

PART I

Congregations

Body Language

"Believe me, fellows, everyone from the Pharaoh on down is an equally valued member of the team."

10

"Excuse me, I'd like to volunteer for committee work involving sensitivity and sacrifice in challenging a secularized, value-impoverished society with the radical claims of the gospel. I have Thursday afternoons free."

"Would you like a word with me, Mrs. Thundermuffin?"

12

"Is this the room that needs a volunteer to help with the church bulletin?"

"I've never been good at repentance, Pastor.
I'll just let you use my condo during August,
and God can call it even."

14

"Toni and I met during this morning's 'Greet Your Neighbor' time. We'd like you to marry us."

Shortly after becoming a father, Pastor Merle Morgan
ponders the mixed blessing of
"Pastor with Cute Kid Syndrome."

"After three weeks of enjoying the church's services, prayer, fellowship, and counseling, I still feel a deep spiritual yearning. So I'm going to sue your socks off."

18

19

"You're in a rut, Rev. Every time I come here you preach
about the resurrection."

20

"Remember us? Wedding in '58,
christenings in '61 and '64 . . . ?"

21

"*Thanks for the marriage counseling, Pastor.*
We feel much better."

"*I think we'd better buy smaller letters
and spell the word out.*"

"You bet it's a gift, and wait till you see what he does
with Lamentations."

"We go to the generic church ... the tithe is only 9 percent."

25

"Today, class, we learn to read a congregation's nonverbal communications while we preach."

"*They have a funny way of greeting first-time visitors around here.*"

27

"It looks like Pastor must have had a hard week."

28

"Actually, Martin, I prefer the term Assistant Pastor.*"*

29

SIGN
LANGUAGE
TRANSLATOR

"... and chief of the Manasseh tribe was Gamaliel the
son of Pedahzur, brother of Ammishaddai...."

"He does this every winter to make us think they haven't turned the thermostat down."

"Herman promised me he'd come to church even when football season started."

"*Ricki is our minister of aerobics.*"

Expansion

©1988 Doug Hall

"Well, I see everybody *has ideas about what they'd like to see in our new building.*"

"Get me the contractor, and hurry!"

37

"*The Flock is coming through on the building fund drive, but not without a good deal of bleating.*"

"Are we glad to hear that you don't know where you'll get the money you need—for a minute there we were afraid you wanted to get it from us."

"Yes, it's quite a nest, but they only use it once a week."

"Today's collection goes toward replacing our pews,
which have been here since 1785."

"I think we ordered the wrong cupola."

"Do you think we're getting a bit too political?"

"What worries me is that this model cost more to build than the present church did."

©1986 Nick Hobart.

44

"They're not going to believe this back home!"

Johnson

"Before we begin our special congregational meeting, let's all stand and sing 'Blest Be the Tie That Binds.' "

Music

"No offense, Henry, but since I'll be preaching on 'Faith and the Nuclear Age,' maybe we should sing something other than 'Leaning on the Everlasting Arms.'"

"*They donated it, but they didn't care for the offertory today.*"

"This song isn't really special to me, but it does provide a wonderful showcase for my voice."

©1986 Mary Chambers

50

"And now, we'll be blessed with a number by the youth percussion ensemble."

"The sopranos and altos will sing 'Hallelujah,' the tenors will sing 'Amen,' and the basses will sing 'Oo-wah, diddle-dee, doo-wah.'"

"...and I got that scar from the chairman of the board during the second battle of 'Guitars in the Sanctuary' back in '71."

53

"Mrs. McNulty's ministry in song has changed somewhat since she started using 'tracks.'"

"I want to request prayer for my brother in the music
ministry, Billy Lee Sanders, who was injured in a
speaker avalanche last week."

"*Let's sing that old favorite, hymn 131 ... with each of us altering the third stanza to suit his or her own views on the Millennium.*"

Boards & Committees

"The chairman of the trustees flipped out, flew to Las Vegas, and gambled away the church. Our new pastor, Eddie 'the Knife' LaRue, is waiting outside."

"Well, gentlemen, I see the hour is late. . . ."

"*Our bylaws specifically state that the will of God cannot be overturned without a two-thirds majority vote.*"

60

"Tough interview?"

© Rob Portlock, 1983.

"Jimmy, we're the Pastor/Parish Relations Committee, and we'd like to ask you a few questions about your dad."

"Now, as your treasurer, when I talk about our going into Chapter 11, I'm not talking about the book of Matthew."

"Pastor Smith wouldn't hold a grudge over a little thing like that ... would he?"

"The committee listed all the qualities needed in an effective youth pastor. I wouldn't let a person like this into my house."

©1986 Doug Hall

65

"I think it's time we look into our church board's activities!"

"This recommendation comes as a recommendation of the personnel committee, the finance committee, and the board of deacons. The church staff has approved it unanimously. We also feel it is the will of God. Is there any discussion?"

"Things seem a little unsettled here after last night's
board meeting, dear."

"I don't care who broke down the walls of Jericho!
I move that we pay for it out of the general fund
and charge it up to miscellaneous."

70

"Now—the board meeting can begin."

"... and when the pastor cut down the bean stalk, the
giant committee came tumbling down, and the church
lived happily ever after."

© Mary Chambers 1985

"For goodness sake, Harvey, are they still after you to join that committee?"

73

"It's a special model for committees ... it comes
equipped with one gas pedal, four steering wheels, and
ten sets of brakes."

"I have a recurring dream in which I have the elders
pleading for mercy; but when I wake up,
I can never remember how!"

"You'll be impressed by our board. They're tops when it comes to decision making."

"Looks like the pastor has found a way to motivate the building committee."

"I told *the search committee their background check didn't go far enough.*"

Christian Education

Armed to the teeth, Sunday school teacher Nat Willowby prepares to do battle with the forces of darkness.

"We interrupt this sermon to inform you that the fourth grade boys are now in complete control of their Sunday school class and are holding Miss Moseby hostage. . . ."

"Who's this 'Amazing Grace' you keep talking about?"

"And a special word of thanks to those of you who helped with our Vacation Bible School."

83

"*But other than that, the youth retreat was a success.*"

"I don't want to be first or last. I want to wallow somewhere in the middle."

85

"Thank you, class, for quieting down and giving me your attention."

"So, Winston, how was the Youth Lock-in?"

"On second thought, Mr. Smith, the King James Version may be just right for you."

"As you can see on your handouts, today's topic is original sin."

"Okay, four-year-olds! Let's polish off
the book of Leviticus!"

90

"No, Francine. Solomon did not have three hundred porcupines."

91

"*Many churches are going to this heavy-duty model to protect their Sunday school chalk.*"

"I see the CE director is training for recruiting
Sunday school teachers for the fall programs."

© Mary Chambers, 1981

Mouton-Chambers

"And a special word of thanks to the men's class for
our floral arrangements...."

94

LEADERSHIP TRAINING

JOHNSON

PART II

Pastors

In the Pulpit

"Pastor always wanted to do that before he retired."

"This year our special Christmas offering will go to cover damages and lawsuits resulting from the donkey running amuck at our living Nativity."

© 1985 Doug Hall.

It occurs to Rev. Billings in the middle of point 2 that point 3 misses the point entirely.

102

"And until next Sunday, remember . . . God loves you,
I love you, and Brother Al here is working on it."

103

"They say it's a tough church to preach at!"

"This is my fourth sermon on the transforming power
of the gospel. Why do you look like
the same old bunch?"

Pastor Dahl lost a button and gained a new
appreciation for pulpit furnishings.

"My text today is 'Take no thought for what ye shall put on.'"

107

"I'm coming to a stopping point in the sermon, if we can all be just a bit more patient."

"This is a great sermon, folks. I feel so convicted I don't think I can finish it."

"It's those credit-check calls that slow everything down."

"Nice to hear a good old-fashioned sermon again, Rev."

"Retired chaplain. Wait till he calls the choir to attention."

"Yes. Yes. I see that hand."

"Nothing personal . . . nothing personal . . . nothing personal. . . ."

116

"Today's sermon is one I've wanted to preach for some time now...."

"No *one falls asleep during* his *sermons.*"

118

"Please excuse the absence of my robe. Until a few
minutes ago, I thought my vacation began today!"

"*Now for the highlights of my sermon.*"

"I left the water running in the baptistry!"

"The pastor certainly put everything he had into
that sermon!"

"These aren't my own statistics. These are the statistics of a man who knows what he's talking about."

123

In the Office

"So I had a couple hours with nothin' to do, so I thought I'd drop in and see you...."

127

"You have a book you'd like me to read, Mrs. Brown?
Why, how thoughtful of you!"

129

"I use it to write all my sermons—it's a parsonal computer."

"Ever have one of those days when you felt you just had to rebuke someone?"

131

"Roadcup, you've got a lot to learn about christening babies!"

© Mary Chambers, 1984.

132

"Rev. Greer refuses to negotiate . . . he said we should talk to his agent."

"Adkins there is pre-trib, Johnson is post-trib, and the fellow with the silly grin on his face stopped studying prophecy years ago."

"Miss Simmons? The program people are at my east door and the building people are at my west door. I'm going to lunch."

"The athletes in the congregation say I should be more athletic. The businessmen say I should be more businesslike. Fred, I admit I'm worried about what you're going to say."

"About my salary—as it was in the beginning, and is
now . . . so shall it be evermore?"

139

"Him? He's my assistant pastor. I believe he is in the process of relating the gospel to the eighties."

141

"While you were out, Constantine converted to Christianity, Luther spearheaded the Reformation, Wesleyan revivals broke out in England, Bryan won the Scopes trial, religious broadcasting swept the nation. . . ."

"Oh, good . . . you're not busy."

"It's somebody from Washington, and they say that our next fifteen converts have got to be Hispanic."

144

"A man from 'Ripley's Believe It or Not!' wants a picture of someone on fire for the Lord."

145

© Doug Hall, 1984.

"It was awesome, Pastor Bob! Right after you left, y'know, everybody else on staff came down with this really gnarly kind of flu. So, anyway, that left me to emcee the Crenshaw funeral last Saturday.... Pastor Bob?"

"How did the singles group respond to your suggestion that they call themselves 'The Leftovers'?"

"Any word yet, Pastor, about my request for a photocopier?"

"Tuesday morning ... ladies' aerobics."

"I can't think of anything to preach on!"

150

At Home

"It's my pop scouting around for sermon illustrations
. . . try to be spontaneous."

"You are coming to church this morning, aren't you?"

153

"Aha! Pastor Hicks, has the Watchdog Committee found you wasting precious time this balmy afternoon?"

154

"*Looks like the pastor's wife isn't used to our social activities yet!*"

156

"It was his last request!"

"Now that you've mastered ministry and management, how about tackling tender loving care?"

© Brenda Burbank, 1980

158

"I have a great idea! Let's reverse things. Today you be grouchy at church and charming at home."

"So how's my bundle of sermon illustrations today?"

160

"*Preaching to a video-taped congregation is* not *a television ministry.*"

162

163

"*Good morning, Reverend Bill! Ain't it good to be here today? Raise your hand and say 'Amen'!*"

"God loves you . . . and everyone else has a wonderful plan for your life."

165

. . . and Abroad

"So you thought you'd get away from the church for a day, huh? Don't you feel guilty? What about all your parishioners? And you call yourself a pastor...."

"Sorry to interrupt the vacation, folks. But your congregation has called twenty-eight times to say they can't find the Communion cups."

"I'm sorry, Reverend, but we do not give clergy
discounts on the Indiana Toll Road."

"This year I'm going to relax and forget about church business! Open me a bottle of sermon"

© Cartoons by Johns, 1980

"No, dear. Today would be the building committee—
so it must be Wednesday."